DELTA PUBLIC LIBRARY
402 MAIN STREET
DELTA, OH 43515

S0-FVK-347
UHL

AR:
PTS: ✗

WITHDRAWN

OCT 0 4 2017

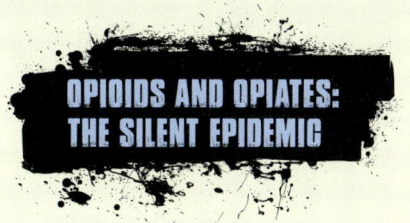

OPIOIDS AND OPIATES: THE SILENT EPIDEMIC

Who Is Using Opioids and Opiates?

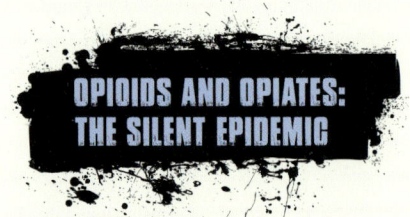

Chronic Pain and Prescription Painkillers
The Dangers of Drug Abuse
The Heroin Crisis
Preventing and Treating Addiction
Who Is Using Opioids and Opiates?

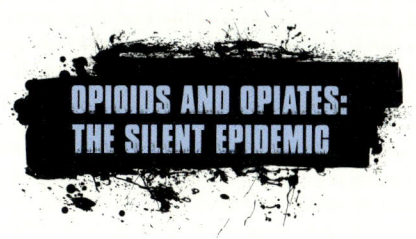

Who Is Using Opioids and Opiates?

XINA UHL

Delta Public Library

Mason Crest
450 Parkway Drive, Suite D
Broomall, PA 19008
www.masoncrest.com

©2018 by Mason Crest, an imprint of National Highlights, Inc.

All rights reserved. No part of this publication may be reproduced or transmitted in any form or by any means, electronic or mechanical, including photocopying, recording, taping, or any information storage and retrieval system, without permission from the publisher.

Printed and bound in the United States of America.

CPSIA Compliance Information: Batch #OPO2017.
For further information, contact Mason Crest at 1-866-MCP-Book.

First printing
1 3 5 7 9 8 6 4 2

Library of Congress Cataloging-in-Publication Data

on file at the Library of Congress
ISBN: 978-1-4222-3827-1 (hc)
ISBN: 978-1-4222-7967-0 (ebook)

OPIOIDS AND OPIATES: THE SILENT EPIDEMIC series ISBN: 978-1-4222-3822-6

QR CODES AND LINKS TO THIRD-PARTY CONTENT

You may gain access to certain third party content ("Third-Party Sites") by scanning and using the QR Codes that appear in this publication (the "QR Codes"). We do not operate or control in any respect any information, products, or services on such Third-Party Sites linked to by us via the QR Codes included in this publication, and we assume no responsibility for any materials you may access using the QR Codes. Your use of the QR Codes may be subject to terms, limitations, or restrictions set forth in the applicable terms of use or otherwise established by the owners of the Third-Party Sites. Our linking to such Third-Party Sites via the QR Codes does not imply an endorsement or sponsorship of such Third-Party Sites, or the information, products, or services offered on or through the Third- Party Sites, nor does it imply an endorsement or sponsorship of this publication by the owners of such Third-Party Sites.

Table of Contents

1: A Different Epidemic 7
2: What Are Opiates 13
3: The Range of Opioids and Opiates 19
4: Avenues to Addiction...29
5: Living as an Addict..39
6: Over and Through Addiction 49

Series Glossary of Key Terms...58
Further Reading 59
Internet Resources 60
Index 62
Photo Credits/About the Author..64

KEY ICONS TO LOOK FOR:

Words to understand: These words with their easy-to-understand definitions will increase the reader's understanding of the text while building vocabulary skills.

Sidebars: This boxed material within the main text allows readers to build knowledge, gain insights, explore possibilities, and broaden their perspectives by weaving together additional information to provide realistic and holistic perspectives.

Educational Videos: Readers can view videos by scanning our QR codes, providing them with additional educational content to supplement the text. Examples include news coverage, moments in history, speeches, iconic sports moments and much more!

Text-dependent questions: These questions send the reader back to the text for more careful attention to the evidence presented there.

Research projects: Readers are pointed toward areas of further inquiry connected to each chapter. Suggestions are provided for projects that encourage deeper research and analysis.

Series glossary of key terms: This back-of-the book glossary contains terminology used throughout this series. Words found here increase the reader's ability to read and comprehend higher-level books and articles in this field.

 **Words to Understand in This Chapter**

junkie—a person addicted to narcotics.
overdose—to take a lethal or toxic amount of a drug.
rehab—a rehabilitation treatment for addicts.

◀ *According to the Centers for Disease Control, 91 Americans die every day from an opioid overdose. On December 15, 2016, one such victim was Jacob DeGroote, a popular student-athlete from Arizona.*

A Different Epidemic

In many ways, he was the ideal American boy. An all-star athlete and academic, he had a longtime girlfriend. He was well-liked and hardworking, juggling two jobs at once. His smile lit up the room.

And at age 20, Jacob DeGroote was dead.

A clean-cut young man from the Phoenix, Arizona suburbs, he didn't look like a *junkie*. It started when someone gave him a pill at school. From there, he took another. And another. Soon, he was using black tar heroin. The smart young man had a 4.2 grade point average. Notre Dame's football program was recruiting him, and he had been offered a full ride at Northern Arizona University. He also had a big problem.

His mother was a nurse in a hospital emergency room. But even she didn't know he was addicted to opiates.

"He didn't want to be an addict," Jacob's mother, Mari DeGroote, said. "He wanted more than anything to get well."

He agreed to a stint in *rehab*.

He said, "I wish I'd never taken that first pill. I never thought I would become addicted. I thought I could be smarter than the pills."

Family problems followed: fights over his drug use and Jacob's parents kicking him out of the house. He went away to rehab and the night he returned home he doubled up on prescription sleep and anxiety medications. His breathing stopped first, then his heart.

Jacob is just one of many victims of drug addiction.

A Growing Epidemic

Since 1999, the number of *overdose* deaths has claimed more than half a million people—quadruple the rate it had been prior to this. The majority of these deaths involve opioids, both prescription opioids and heroin. Once an inner city, low-income user problem, the scourge of opioid abuse has moved into the suburbs. Now it affects the lives of Americans both rich and poor, urban and rural. It respects no ethnic or cultural differences. Abusers range from pre-teens to the elderly, from one end of the United States to the other.

Opioid addiction has become more than a set of sobering statistics. It has become an epidemic, one which continues to claim lives, destroy families, and crowd jails and prisons due to users who steal and commit worse crimes to feed their habits. It overwhelms hospital emergency rooms, and costs employers millions in lost productivity.

The Scope of the Problem

The problem shows no signs of slowing down. In its most recent report, issued in 2016, the Centers for Disease Control reported that statistically significant increases in death rates

An Equal Opportunity Addiction

On April 21, 2016, 57-year-old music icon Prince was found unresponsive in his Minnesota home. Shortly thereafter, he died. While the world mourned the loss of his musical genius, questions arose. What happened? The day before his death, an opioid addiction specialist had been called in to help him. It was too late. The medical examiner's office conducted toxicology tests which revealed that the singer died from an accidental overdose of the opioid fentanyl.

Celebrities are not the only ones to suffer from addiction. Michelle, a suburban mother from Portsmouth, Virginia, once spent her days packing school lunches and helping her children with their homework. But then a pain prescription for a toothache opened her to the world of drug abuse. Sometimes she took up to 60 pills a day. She went from doctor to doctor asking for prescriptions to feed her habit. She bought opioids off the Internet, and finally on the street. Street drugs drew her into addiction to heroin, crack cocaine, and crystal meth. She abandoned her family six years later. "The disease got a hold of me more. I didn't care about anything but the drugs," she later said. "At the time, drugs were becoming more and more the center of my life."

Eventually, Michelle was able to successfully end her dependence on drugs. But she is careful to explain that she must always be on her guard against relapse. If she doesn't, she could be one of the fatality statistics herself.

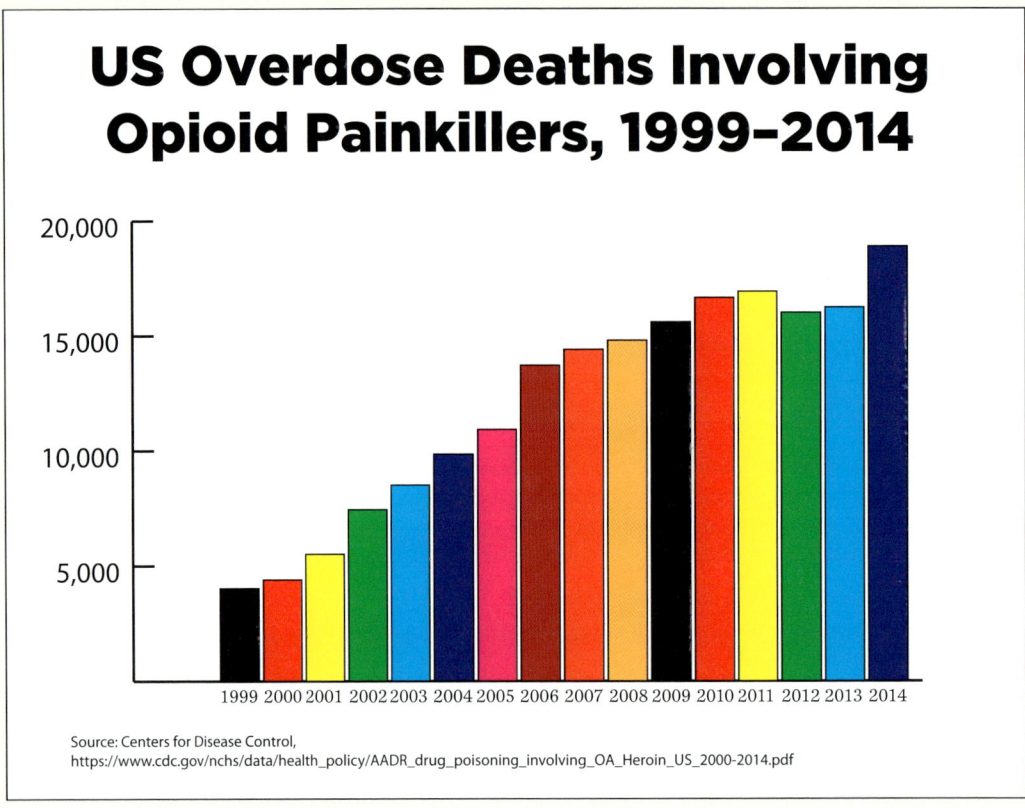

due to opioid abuse occurred in a number of states: Maine, 26.2 percent; Connecticut, 25.6 percent; Maryland, 20.1; New Hampshire, 30.9 percent; New Jersey; Rhode Island; Kentucky, 21.1 percent; and Florida, 22.7 percent. Predictions from Columbia University experts state that overdose deaths may peak in 2017, though they are not predicted to fall until 2034.

In 2016, President Barack Obama issued a proclamation for the Prescription Opioid and Heroin Epidemic Awareness Week, which took place from September 18 through September 26. He called for increased awareness and funding for this public health crisis. Clearly, opioid-related abuse is not going anywhere soon. The pages that follow will focus on what opioids do, how they work, who suffers from the epidemic, and how it happens. You'll learn about a drug that has been around for hundreds of years in various forms. And about the latest developments in synthetic opioid production and distribution.

Despite the frightening statistics and serious health consequences from addiction, there is hope for recovery. While avoiding drug use to begin with is the easiest and best solution, we will also cover the range of options for recovery from this difficult problem.

Text-Dependent Questions

1. How has opioid abuse changed from the past to the present?
2. How does opioid addiction impact the community?
3. Has opioid addiction topped out or is it continuing to rise?

Research Project

What does the opioid addiction problem look like in your local community? For this research project, you will research what is happening. Three sources of information are necessary. These can be articles from the local or state newspapers, news videos about the problem, statements from law enforcement and medical personnel, even interviews with your school administrators or counselors. Ask: is opioid abuse a problem here? How has drug addiction changed over the last few years? What is being done to educate people about drugs?

When you are finished, write a one page essay about what you found. Be sure to list your sources at the end of your essay.

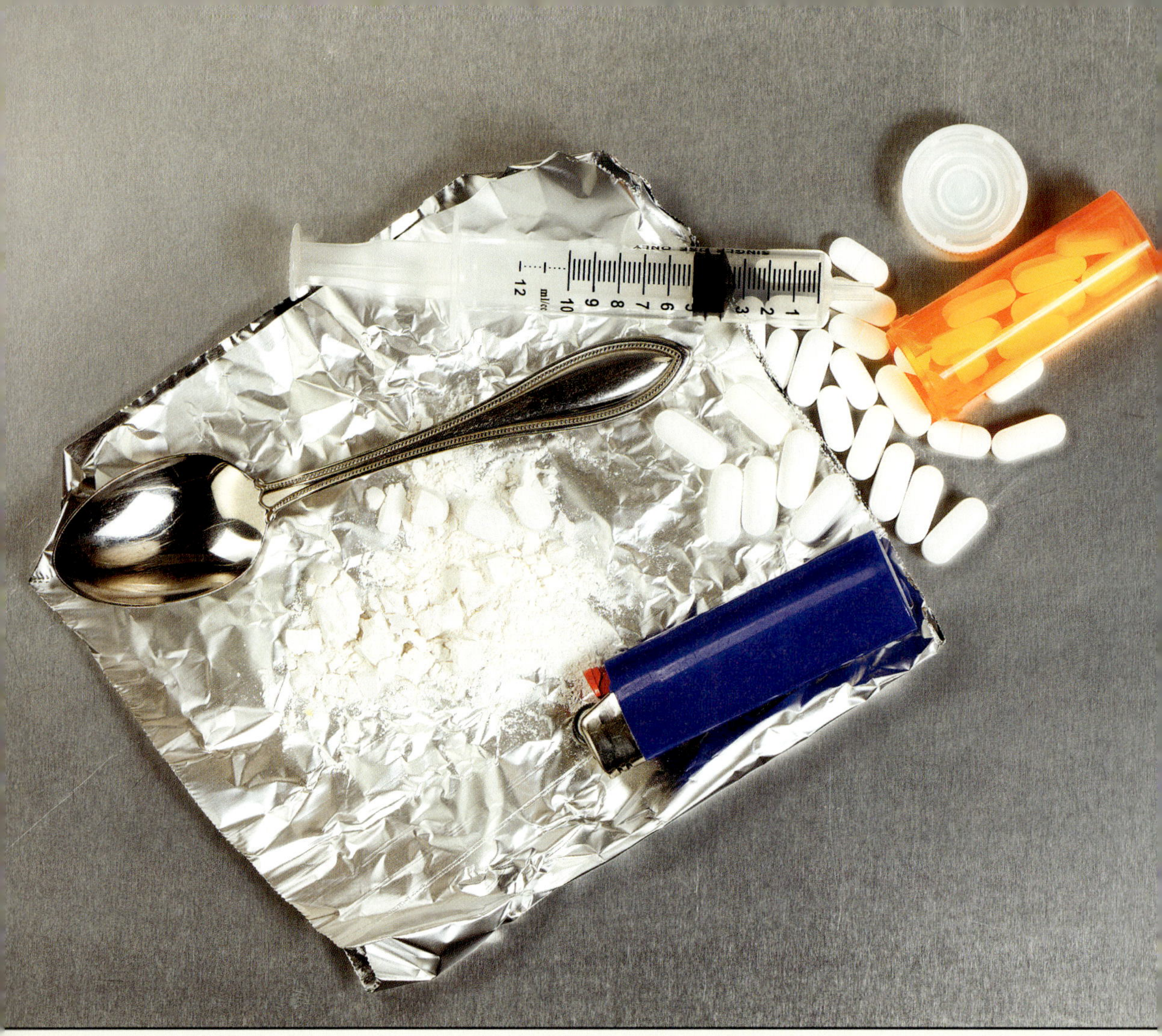

 **Words to Understand in This Chapter**

derive—to take from a certain source.
euphoria—an intense feeling of well-being.
narcotic—a drug that dulls the senses, relieves pain, and can cause stupor, coma, or death.
synthesize—to produce something from another source.

◀ *Opiates are a class of drugs that are derived from natural sources, such as the sap of the opium poppy,* **Papaver somniferum.** *This plant grows naturally in Asia and Europe. Opiates come in many different forms, including pills, powders, and liquids.*

2

What Are Opiates?

Poppies are pretty flowers popular in gardens. The California state flower is a poppy, a certain strain that is orange. Opium poppies, though, have a powerful *narcotic* hidden in their seed pods. These delicate flowers bloom in red, white, or purple in a hot climate. When the flower petals fall off, cuts in seed pods produce a milky sap. This sap contains the narcotic known as opium. Raw opium is formed into lumps or cakes that can be dried out into powder. For centuries, opium was used as a powerful painkiller—one of the few effective drugs. Practitioners smoked it, ate it, or drank it in a sort of tea. It was used to soothe the pain of internal bleeding, broken bones, coughs, cancer, childbirth, and toothaches. Other conditions such as insomnia, anxiety, and fear before battle also responded well to the treatment.

 **Opium Through the Ages**

Five thousand years ago, ancient people from Assyria and Sumeria were the first to use opium. They called the opium poppy *hul gil*, which means "joy plant." They may have discovered opium's narcotic properties by observing cattle that became intoxicated after eating the plant's seed pods. Clay tablets from 2000 BCE recommend a potion of crushed poppies and fly droppings to help calm unhappy children.

Cultivation of the plant spread eastward into Greece. By the seventh century CE it reached China. There, it was taken in a pill form or mixed into beverages. Arab traders introduced opium west as far as Spain and north as far as Vienna by the ninth century CE. As Columbus explored the seas in the fifteenth century one of the items he was tasked with bringing home was opium. In 1680, a British physician named Thomas Sydenham bottled opium, calling it laudanum. It grew popular across Europe. Europeans began to smoke opium after the introduction of tobacco from Native Americans. Soon, most people smoked it. In the eighteenth century, opium abuse became such a widespread problem in China that the government outlawed its use. Two trade wars fought between Britain and China became known as the Opium Wars.

Almost all painkillers contained opium by the nineteenth century. Morphine was synthesized from opium in 1804; this drug is ten times more potent than opium. The newly invented hypodermic syringe was used to inject it. Its use on hundreds of thousands of wounded soldiers during the Civil War produced untold numbers of addicts. Heroin was derived in 1874. The dangers of addiction led many governments to pass laws to prohibit its use except by physicians.

Users reported *euphoria* and a sense of calm and peacefulness. It allowed people to heal with less pain. Still, today, drugs *derived* from the opium poppy serve as painkillers.

But there is a dark side to this wonder drug, too. Some users don't want to stop taking it. After regular use they soon find it necessary to increase their dosage to achieve the same effects. Stopping the drug results in unpleasant withdrawal physical symptoms: severe headaches, uncontrolled trembling, chills, muscle and bone pain, insomnia, diarrhea, muscle spasms, and vomiting. Some people experience nightmares, hallucinations, and depression. Emotional symptoms can be just as difficult to handle. These symptoms include an intense desire for the drug and fear of losing its positive effects, an inability to conceive of continuing to live without it.

How Do Opiates and Opioids Work?

The word *opioids* refers to an entire class of drugs that both contain or are derived from opium and those that have the same properties but are not derived from them. For instance, heroin is both an opioid and an opiate, or drugs that contain or are derived from opium. They tend to encourage sleep and

 **Educational Video**

To watch a documentary on the "Opium Wars" between China and Great Britain, scan here:

>  **Did You Know?**
>
> Muscle spasms from opium withdrawal result in involuntary kicking movements. This is where the term "kicking the habit" came from.

relieve pain. However, drugs that are *synthesized* to be similar to the poppy plant's narcotic properties, but do not contain any actual narcotic from the plant are opioids, but not opiates.

The residue in opium that serves as a drug is known as an alkaloid. They make up about 10 percent of the weight of raw opium. Opium alkaloids are divided into two types depending on their chemical structures. One type works on the central nervous system. They relieve pain, act as a narcotic, and have addictive properties. Examples of these are morphine, codeine, and thebaine. The second type of opium alkaloids only act to relax the smooth, involuntary muscles of the body. Examples are papaverine and noscapine (also called narcotine).

Opioids are similar to chemicals in the brain and body that attach to parts of nerve cells called opioid receptors. Three types of opioid receptors exist. Named after letters from the Greek alphabet, they are called mu, delta, and kappa. Each of these three receptors has different actions in the body. Mu receptors are associated with the pleasurable and pain-relieving effects of opioids.

Opioids act on three primary places in the brain and nervous system. The limbic system controls emotions. Opioids create sensations of pleasure, contentment, and ease. The brainstem is the source of automatic brain functions such as breathing. Opioids reduce pain, stop coughing, and slow down respiration. The spinal cord recognizes sensations from the body, then sends them to the brain. Opioids work in this area to decrease pain as well.

The brain makes natural versions of opioids which are referred to as endogenous opioids. They also attached to your brain's opioid receptors. They help the body control pain. They also release natural chemicals called endorphins which cause relaxation.

Text-Dependent Questions

1. What part of the opium poppy contains the narcotic substance the plant is famous for?
2. What are the two types of opium alkaloids?
3. What is the relationship between the brain's receptors and opium alkaloids?

Research Project

By rereading the chapter and consulting reputable web pages and library books, compile a list of at least 10 effects that opiates and opioids have on the body. Then, either print out a picture of a human body from the internet or draw one. Draw arrows to point out the areas affected.

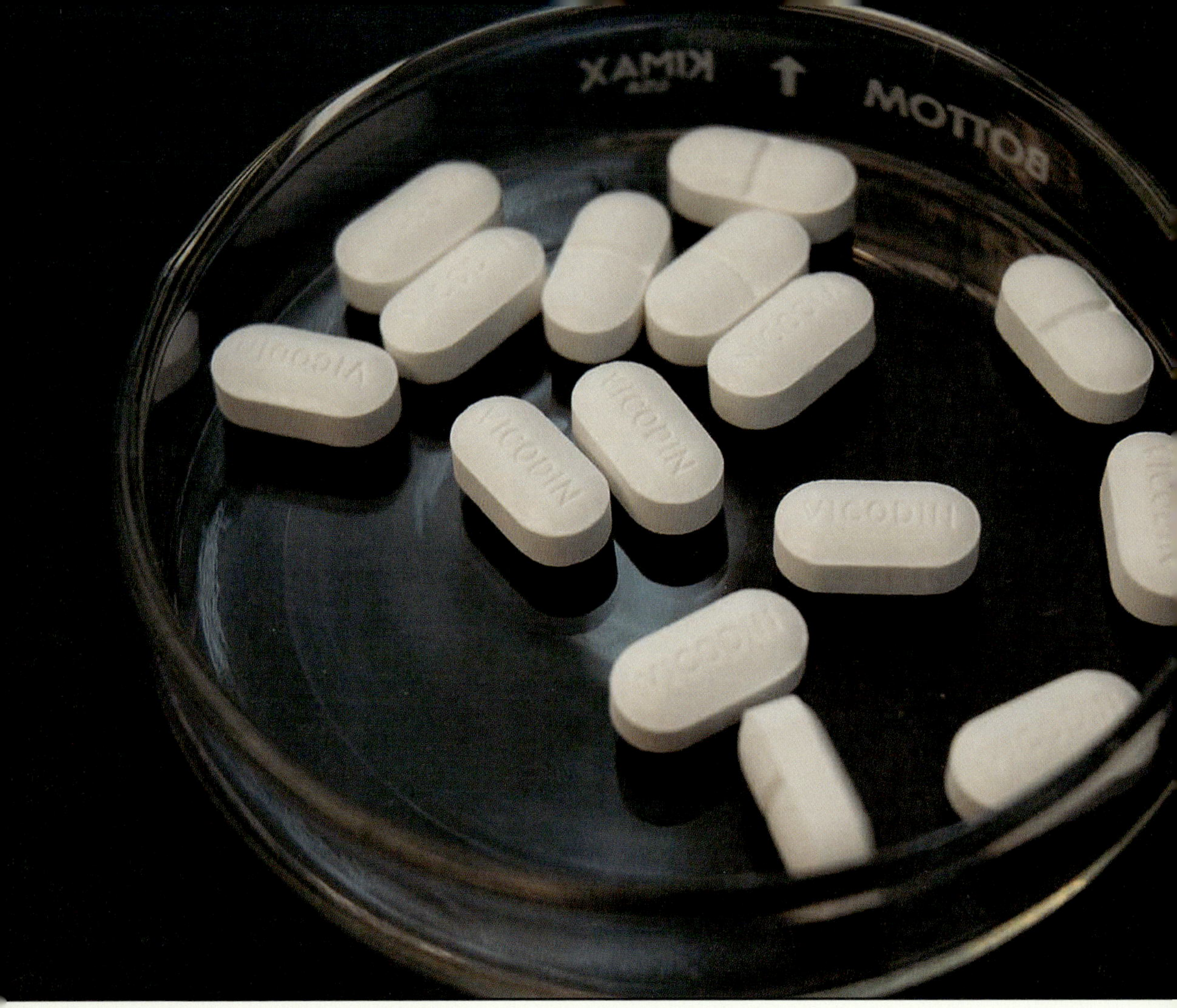

 **Words to Understand in This Chapter**

fraudulent—deceitful or illegal.

generic drug—copies of brand name drugs that are usually less expensive.

methamphetamine—a stimulant with the chemical compound C10H15N that has both medical and illegal uses.

semisynthetic—chemically altering a natural material

suppository—a solid medicine designed to be inserted into the rectum, where it melts.

Some people inaccurately refer to all drugs as narcotics. Only natural, synthetic, or semisynthetic opioids can be properly classified as narcotic drugs. Pictured here is hydrocodone, an opioid pain medication sold under the trade name Vicodin.

The Range of Opioids and Opiates

Since the use of the opium poppy came into being many drugs have resulted from them. Some are derived directly from opium. These are morphine, codeine, heroin, thebaine, and orpivaine. Synthetic opioids include: demerol, fentanyl, dilaudid, norco, lortab, atarax, methadone, and buprenorphine. Some synthetic opioids are used to treat opioid addiction, and include naloxone and naltrexone. Other drugs are *semisynthetic*. These are oxymorphone and OxyContin (containing thebaine), hydrocodone (containing codeine), and hydromorphone (containing morphine). Be aware that many brand name drugs, such as demerol, are also prescribed as *generic drugs*. Generic drugs are copies of brand-name drugs. The generic drug for demerol is meperidine, oxycodone hydrochloride is the generic name for OxyContin, Vicodin is the brand-name for a mixture of drugs including acetaminophen (not an opioid) and hydrocodone (an opioid), and so on.

Opium

A substance that is extracted from an opium poppy, opium is the source of many narcotics. All opium that is used legally is imported from other countries who must follow regulations for growth. Available as a liquid, solid, or powder, it can be smoked, injected or taken in a pill. It is often combined with marijuana or *methamphetamines*.

How potent opium's effects are depends on how high the dose is and whether it is taken orally or via smoking or injection. Smoked opium works quickly because the chemicals are absorbed into the lungs and sent immediately to the brain. Oral doses must be processed through the digestive system, which takes longer to work. Overdose effects include slow breathing, dizziness, seizures, weakness, unconsciousness leading to coma and death.

Morphine

One of the most effective painkillers, morphine is derived from the opium poppy's narcotic properties. Most of the morphine used in the United States is processed into codeine and other derivatives. It can be taken in oral doses, tablets, capsules, *suppositories*, and injections. People dependent on the drug tend to prefer injections because it takes effect more quickly. It effects the body by relieving pain, decreasing hunger, and reducing

An Afghan farmer holds the seed pod of an opium poppy. Juice from the seed pod can be refined into pain-killing opiates like morphine, codeine, and heroin.

coughing. Overdosers experience slowed breathing, pulse rate, and lowered pulse rate. Coma and death can result.

Heroin

One of the most highly addictive and dangerous drugs in the opioid family is heroin. It is processed from morphine, which occurs naturally in the seed pod of the opium poppy. These crops are grown in Southeast Asia, Southwest Asia (in particular, Afghanistan), Mexico, and Colombia. "Black tar" heroin is found primarily in the western United States and has its ori-

(Top) A chunk of black tar heroin. The drug's sticky texture is due to the way it is processed. (Bottom) Heroin is often sold on the streets as a white or brown powder. The two varieties pictured here were smuggled into the US from Asia.

gin in Mexico. It looks like a black sticky paste. White heroin is found primarily on the East Coast of the United States, and comes from Colombia. It is usually sold as a white or brown powder.

Heroin is not available through legal sources. People obtain it "on the street." Usually, this street heroin is mixed with, or "cut" with either other drugs or white powdered substances such as sugar, powdered milk, quinine, or starch. Sales of pure heroin, while becoming more popular, is still uncommon. Heroin that is particularly pure is usually snorted or smoked. Other types can be injected, snorted, or smoked.

Heroin enters the brain rapidly, creating a "rush" or intense euphoria which tapers off into a half-asleep state. Other symptoms of use include heaviness in the limbs, nausea, skin flushing, dry mouth, constricted pupils, and depression of the respiratory system.

Addiction to heroin can occur quickly. Regular use builds up the body's tolerance to it. The abuser must then take more of the drug in order to get the same high. Over time this results in serious physical and emotional dependence, or addiction.

Overdose frequently leading to death is a significant risk with heroin use because of the substances it is usually cut with. Symptoms of an overdose includes slow, shallow breathing, blue fingernails and lips, cold, clammy skin, convulsions, and in the most serious cases, coma and death.

Hydromorphone

This opioid is two to eight times more potent than morphine, though it does not last as long. While it is a legal drug in the US, abusers usually obtain it by forging doctor's prescriptions or by visiting numerous doctors in order to obtain prescriptions. This is known as "doctor shopping." It is also obtained from friends and acquaintances and even outright theft.

The usual form of administration is by tablets. However, injection is also possible by crushing the tablets and dissolving them in a solution. This is taken as a substitute for heroin. The drug produces euphoria, sedation, and relaxation. It can reduce anxiety and result in mood changes, agitation, and impaired thinking. By working in the brain it reduces pain and suppresses coughs.

A number of side effects can occur from use: dizziness, constipation, nausea, vomiting, appetite loss, rash, changes in heart rate, depression of respiratory system, and changes in blood pressure. Pupils may be dilated as well. Overdose results in sleepiness leading to a stupor or coma, cold, clammy skin, severe slowing of respiration, and reduction in blood pressure and heart rate.

Hydromorphone is highly addictive both physically and psychologically.

Methadone

During World War II, scientists synthesized methadone to combat a morphine shortage. It comes in tablets, discs, oral liquid, an injectable solution. Methadone is often provided by drug detox and maintenance facilities in order to treat opioid addiction. It produces drowsiness, sweating, and itchy skin. Abuse leads to tolerance and physical dependency. Withdrawal occurs when use is stopped. This leads to cramps in the abdomen, tremors, nausea, diarrhea, vomiting, and anxiety. When users overdose they suffer from depressed respiration, blue lips and fingernails, spasms in the stomach, weak pulse, convulsions, and may lead to coma and death.

Oxycodone

Like methodone, oxycodone is a synthesized opioid. Under the brand name OxyContin, it is widely abused. It comes in tablets with multiple dosages. Products such as aspirin and acetaminophen are sometimes combined with it. It can also be taken via injection. Tablets are sometimes crushed and sniffed or dissolved in water and injected. Another method of use is to heat a tablet on a piece of aluminum foil and then inhale the smoke from it. The most common effects are euphoria and relaxation. Other effects include pain relief, depression of respiration, constipation, and relief from coughing. Overdose produces sleepiness, weakness, confusion, cold, clammy skin, slowdown of breathing and and heart rate, leading to coma and possible death.

OxyContin is prescribed in a range of strengths, from 10 milligrams to the potent 80 milligram tablets pictured here.

Fentanyl

In 1949, Dr. Paul Janssen developed a synthetic opioid called fentanyl. Because it is 80 times more powerful than morphine it became a popular form of pain relief by doctors. Anesthetics were derived from it and in the 1990s a patch was developed that could transmit the drug through the skin. Patients with chronic cancer pain are one example of those who benefit from

 ### Educational Video

Scan here to see a video with personal stories from addicts and their loved ones.

A bag of Fentanyl pills seized in a DEA raid. Because Fentanyl causes effects similar to heroin, the two drugs are sometimes mixed when sold illegally in order to increase the potency of low-grade heroin. However, including too much Fentanyl in the mix can lead to a deadly overdose, as the drug is much stronger than heroin.

this patch. Tablets are used, too. The Actiq lollipop is effective in long-term pain relief. Other products are a fizzing lozenge and a spray. The patch is most widely used. Drug abusers remove the gel from the patches and either eat the contents or inject them. Patches can also be frozen, cut into pieces, and put under the tongue where the drug is absorbed through the mucus membranes.

In 2015, Fentanyl was prescribed more than six million times for legal use in pain reduction. Illegal distribution is also prevalent and obtained by theft and *fraudulent* prescriptions. Criminal laboratories also manufacture it.

Fentanyl is 50 to 100 times stronger than heroin or morphine. Abuse occurs due to the intense euphoria it creates. In addition to pain relief, other effects are muscle tightness, nausea, vomiting, itching, and depression of the respiratory system. Fentanyl may also function as a direct substitute for heroin addicted individuals. This substitution comes with substantial risks, though. Because of its potency it often results in overdoses that lead to death.

Text-Dependent Questions

1. What are semisynthetic drugs?
2. How are the overdose effects of the drugs profiled in this chapter similar?

Research Project

Locate at least three websites that rank the harmfulness of illegally abused drugs. Using information from these sites, determine the five most dangerous drugs in the United States today. Note how many of the drugs on this list are opioids.

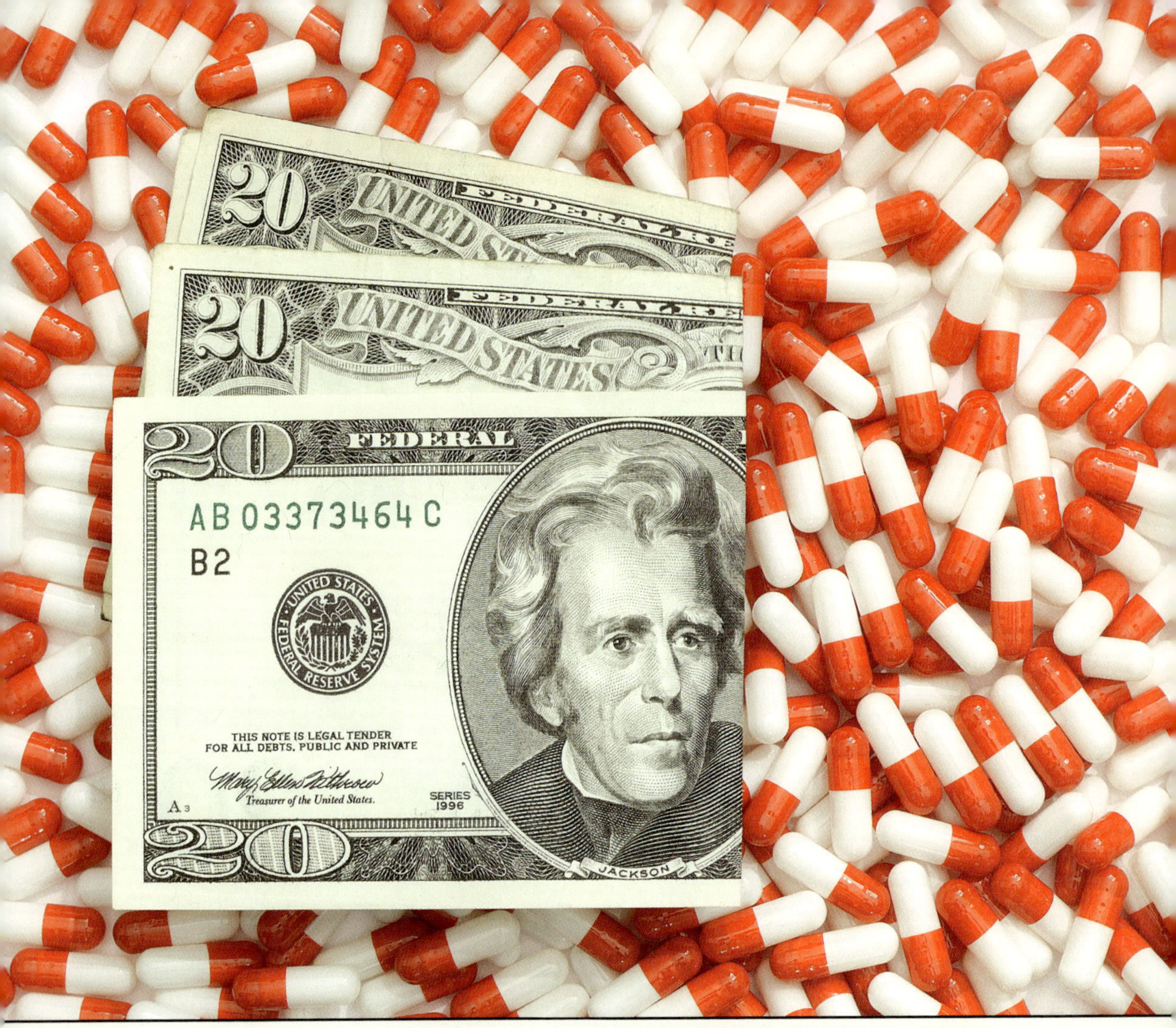

Words to Understand in This Chapter

controlled substance—a drug whose manufacture, possession, and use is subject to government regulations.

pharmaceutical—involved in the manufacturing of medicines.

primary care—health care administered by doctors or nurses at the general level, as opposed to specialists for certain conditions.

relapse—to return to abusing drugs or alcohol.

◀ *Illicit drug sales are a lucrative business, but there is a serious danger when it comes to opioids. In one recent year, the National Institute on Drug Abuse reports there were over 13,600 unintentional deaths caused by overdoses of opioid pain relievers. This made up approximately 83 percent of the total unintentional overdose deaths from all prescription drugs.*

Avenues to Addiction

In February 2013, Alejandro Prosper, also known as "Pun," began a drug trafficking organization with several other conspirators. Prosper, of New Haven, Connecticut, and other members of the group obtained personal identifications of more than 50 medical practitioners. They then used this information in order to create fake prescriptions for oxycodone. Persons called "runners" were used to fill the prescriptions at pharmacies throughout Connecticut. The DEA reports that, "Investigators identified more than 800 fraudulent prescriptions passed by members of the organization using more than 270 different "patient" names." The costs of the prescriptions were usually billed to Medicaid, since most of the runners held state-sponsored medical insurance.

Prosper and his conspirators then sold the oxycodone pills for $20-$30 per milligram. By doing this, the group obtained 80,000 plus pills.

DEA officials charged 11 people in the conspiracy. In January 2017, Prosper pleaded guilty to one count of conspiracy to distribute oxycodone and was sentenced to 57 months in prison, with an additional four years of supervised release.

 **Cruelty to Animals**

At first, Kentucky veterinarian Chad Bailey treated Heather D. Pereira's four-year-old retriever dog like his other patients. He stitched shut the dog's wounds and prescribed the opioid medication Tramadol for pain. Three days later, Pereira visited the vet's office again, claiming that her child had flushed the medicine down the toilet. By the time she returned for a third visit, Bailey was suspicious. He noticed that the dog's wounds were too clean. "Not the sort of cuts you see in nature," he said. Bailey called the police as Periera waited in the office. She was convicted of drug-seeking, or trying to obtain narcotics or other drugs through fraud.

In 2016, near Portland, Oregon, authorities seized 100,000 tramadol pills. They also rescued 17 dogs in filthy living conditions. Four people were arrested for running an opioid distribution ring disguised as a dog breeding business. Deputy Micah Hibpshman of the Clackamas County Police Department believes that the dog business gave them the idea to distribute tramadol.

Across the country, veterinarians are being urged to carefully evaluate the opioids they prescribe to patients and be on the lookout for suspicious behavior.

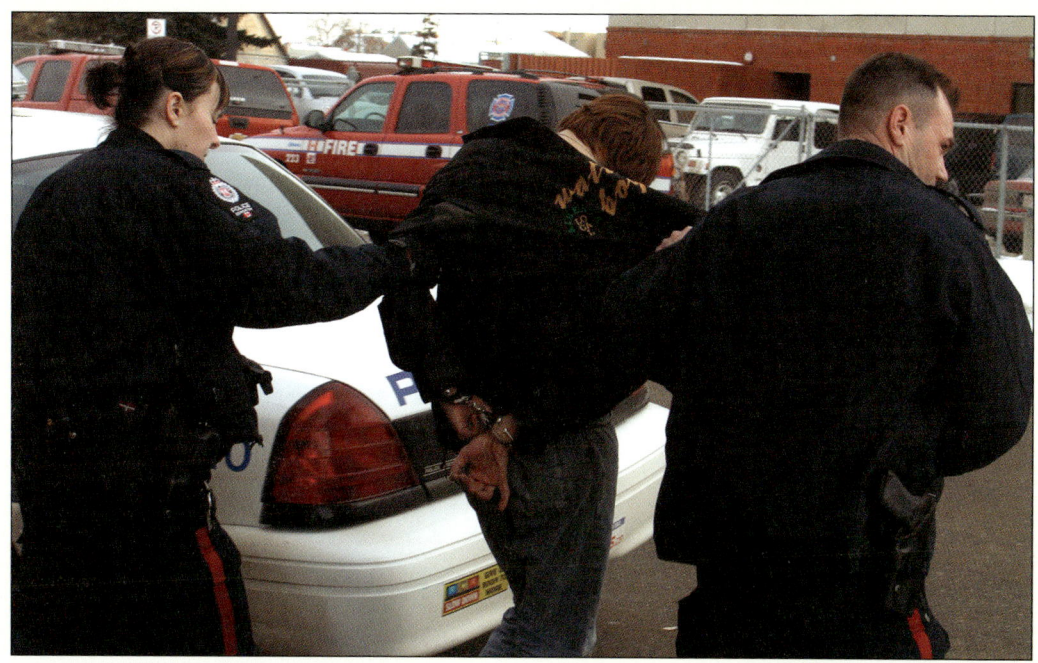

Canadian police arrest a man for illegally distributing drugs in Edmonton, Canada. The opioid epidemic is not confined to the United States, as neighboring countries like Canada and Mexico are also dealing with this public health problem.

The Bigger They Are, the Harder They Fall

Prosper's scheme is only one way that individuals involved in the illegal drug trade work to obtain drugs to sell. But even major *pharmaceutical* companies have been implicated in wrongdoing.

McKesson is the largest drug distributor in the United States, and the fifth-largest company overall. In January 2017 they agreed to pay a record $150 million fine to settle claims that they violated federal law. They also agreed to suspend sales of *controlled substances* from four distribution centers.

In recent years, even some major American pharmaceutical companies have been implicated in schemes to illegally distribute opioids. Pharmaceutical companies also funded two non-profit organizations—the American Academy of Pain Management and the American Pain Society—that lobbied doctors to prescribe opioid pain relievers.

The Justice Department accused McKesson of neglecting to implement an effective means of identifying suspicious orders from pharmacies of powerful painkillers such as oxycodone and hydrocodone. The Controlled Substances Act mandates that they take this action. The fine is the largest to date.

This was not the first time that McKesson had gotten into trouble with the law for selling drugs illegally. In 2008, McKesson was fined $13.25 million for similar breaches of the law.

Do No Harm

As you can see, fraudulent prescriptions and the ability to obtain drugs illegally through pharmacies is big business. Pharmacies are just one link in the chain of opioid abuse, though. Abuse often starts in what is supposed to be the safest place for people's well-being—the doctor's office.

On November 8, 2013, *The New Yorker* reports that two studies in the 1980s assured physicians that narcotics could be prescribed with little risk of patients becoming addicted. Sales marketing by pharmaceutical companies encouraged doctors to prescribe narcotics for pain. As a result, doctors began to increase the amount of narcotics they prescribed to patients. Dentists have also become frequent prescribers of opioids such as Vicodin and Percocet to deal with dental pain. James Hatzell of Collingswood, New Jersey was one of those patients. As a junior in high school, he was prescribed Vicodin for dental surgery. Because he received a prescription from a dentist the opioid seemed less dangerous and more legitimate. It was that prescription that led him down a path to addiction. That path ended when he was arrested in college for dealing drugs. Luckily, Hatzell is in recovery for addiction now.

 **Educational Video**

To see a video on the horrors of drug addiction, scan here:

Doctors and dentists both are being urged to limit the prescription of opioids due to the epidemic of addiction. In 2016, the CDC released updated opioid prescription guidelines targeting *primary care* doctors. These guidelines help medical personnel to look for alternatives to opioids assess the risks of prescribing them, and control their use for long-term conditions.

One Story Among Many

Research published in 2013 by the Substance Abuse and Mental Health Services Administration (SAMHSA) reveals that about 80 percent of prescription painkiller abuse and heroin abuse began with a legitimate prescription for pain medication. Those prescriptions may not come from an ethical doctor, however. Take the story of twenty-year-old Connor Brennan from Fairfax, an affluent suburb of Washington. When Connor was 15, he started smoking marijuana. When his stepbrother explained how he smoked OxyContin, Connor was curious. He tried it.

"It's an instant warm sensation throughout your body—calming, tranquil," Brennan told the *Washington Post*. He immediately thought, "I need to do this as much as possible."

He learned about a local doctor who would supply him with OxyContin prescriptions for $100. At 16, he began regularly using the drugs. He did not think he would get hooked. After all, he was a good student with a loving family and plans for college in the future. But the drugs took over.

He went to a residential treatment center, but got high again as soon as he graduated from it. Soon he was hooked on heroin. At 19, the constant struggle to avoid withdrawal sent him to the emergency room. Again, his parents signed him up for a treatment program. The night he entered treatment his good friend, Madison Walker, overdosed on heroin. He died

Drug	Street Names
Heroin	Big H, Black Tar, Chiva, Hell Dust, Horse, Negra, Smack, and Thunder.
Hydromorphone	D, Dillies, Dust, Footballs, Juice, and Smack.
Methadone	Amidone, Chocolate Chip Cookies, Fizzies, Maria, Pastora, Salvia, Street Methadone, and Wafer.
Morphine	Dreamer, Emsel, First Line, God's Drug, Hows, M.S., Mister Blue, Morf, Morpho, and Unkie.
Opium	Ah-pen-yen, Aunti, Aunti Emma, Big O, Black Pill, Chandoo, Chandu, Chinese Molasses, Chinese Tobacco, Dopium, Dover's Powder, Dream Gun, Dream Stick, Dreams, Easing Powder, Fi-do-nie, Gee, God's Medicine, Gondola, Goric, Great Tobacco, Guma, Hop/hops, Joy Plant, Midnight Oil, Mira, O, O.P., Ope, Pen Yan, Pin Gon, Pox, Skee, Toxy, Toys, When-shee, Ze, and Zero.
Oxycodone	Hillbilly Heroin, Kicker, oC, ox, Roxy, Perc, and oxy.

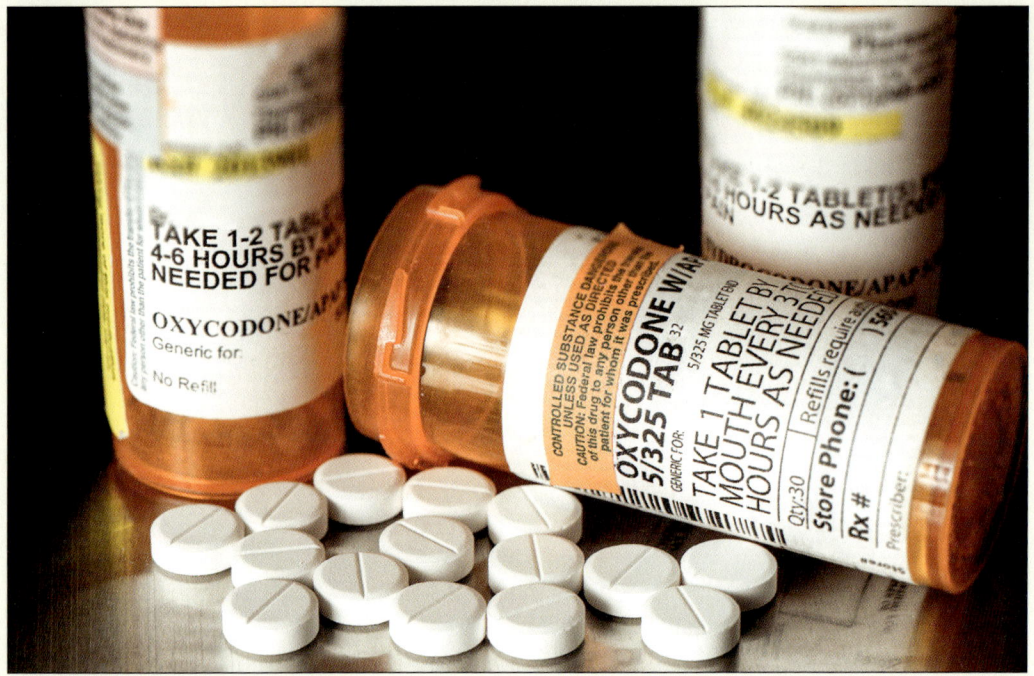

Addiction to opioids often begins with a legitimate prescription of one of these drugs.

with the needle in his arm. Walker had previously gotten clean, just like Brennan. But *relapse* is a constant possibility for former drug addicts.

"You're going to end up dead if you keep using," Connor Brennan advised. "That's the only thing that happens."

Brennan's future is uncertain, like that of so many others who abuse opioids.

On the Street and Off It

Prescription drugs, whether they are obtained legally or illegally, are usually the gateway to other opioid drug use. Once abusers have exhausted options for opioids through medical professionals, they look to purchase it elsewhere. They find it from shady internet sites, friends or acquaintances at school or work, or buying them off the street from drug dealers. Illegal sources of opioids arrive in the US from worldwide criminal organizations, particularly from Mexico and China. In *Dreamland the Story of America's New Opiate Epidemic*, author Sam Quinones argues that increasing legalization of marijuana in the US has led directly to has led to a decline in marijuana sales in Mexico. The drug cartels there have turned to planting opium poppies from which heroin is derived. They also manufacture fentanyl in order to boost sales.

Text-Dependent Questions

1. How do most opioid addictions start?
2. What factors led to an increase in narcotics prescriptions since the 1980s?

Research Project

Using the internet, research a settlement that Purdue Pharma, the maker of OxyContin, has been required to pay the state of Kentucky due to a lawsuit. Reference more than one article about the lawsuit. Then write up a two paragraph essay summarizing the alleged wrongdoing and the actions Purdue Pharma agreed to take.

Words to Understand in This Chapter

domestic violence—violent behavior in the home, usually involving spouses.
illicit—against the law.
incarceration—to live in prison.
shrooms—short for mushrooms with hallucinogenic properties.

The National Institute on Drug Abuse estimates that between 26 million and 36 million people abuse opioids worldwide, with an estimated 2.1 million people in the United States suffering from substance use disorders related to prescription opioid pain relievers.

Living as an Addict

When Deon was only three years old, he remembers his mother lying passed out drunk on the couch. He tried to wake her up because he was hungry, but she just slept on. Deon's home life was chaotic. His mother's boyfriend would hit both of them frequently. The police came more than once. He hung out on the streets as much as possible.

He started drinking at age ten. He liked how it helped him to forget his problems. Then he took harder drugs like heroin. Shooting up made him feel on top of the world. Coming down from the high wasn't as much fun. He would spend hours half asleep. Before long he needed a hit just to get by. Withdrawal was torture. Deon described it as, "It's like I was dying in every awful way you could think of, all at once. Pain in all my bones, throwing up, chills, and I couldn't sleep for days."

He was arrested for buying heroin more than once. A judge put him in a drug treatment program. But Deon was angry and defiant and wanted nothing to do with it. Then he overdosed and ended up in the hospital. Frightened, he entered a halfway house with a substance abuse treatment program. There, he went to a lot of classes and Narcotics Anonymous (NA) meetings to help him live without drugs. He also started taking methadone in order to help him stay off heroin.

Deon said, "Heroin has been hard on my body. I have scars all over my arms, and my kidneys aren't working well. But I'm feeling a little more interested in life these days."

The New Face of Addiction

In many ways, Deon represents the stereotype of a junkie as a low-income minority male living in an inner city ghetto. That stereotype is no longer true, though. Heroin addiction cuts across the US and affects males, females, young, and old. As FBI Director James B. Comey said in 2014, "Heroin today is an urban thing and a suburban thing. It's a black and white thing,

 **Educational Video**

Scan here to watch at video produced by federal law-enforcement agencies that details the life of an opiate addict.

Today, those addicted to opioids are more likely to be successful members of the middle class living in the suburbs than they are to be the stereotypical "junkie" living in squalid conditions in American inner cities.

a rich and poor thing. It's everywhere and everybody."

Increasingly, women are taking the center stage in opioid addiction. The National Institute on Drug Abuse (NIDA) reports that while men tend to have higher rates of use of *illicit* drugs and alcohol than women, women are just as likely to become addicted as men are.

There are significant differences between men and women who use heroin. Women tend to use heroin at a younger age and are less likely to inject it. They tend to use smaller amounts of the drug for a shorter time period.

According to the Centers for Disease Control, every three minutes, a woman in the United States visits the emergency room due to prescription painkiller abuse.

Studies have indicated that prescription opioids affect women differently than men. Women tend to be more sensitive to pain than men, and more likely to visit doctors for help. Both conditions leads to a higher prescription rate for women.

Women have more complex needs than men when it comes to reproductive and hormonal interactions with drugs. Often women have child care concerns. Pregnancy and opiate use is a serious problem as well, since the child may be born with an addiction.

Young white females are abusing opioids like never before. Blake Landry of Arizona is an example. She started smoking marijuana at 16 years of age. Soon she was doing *shrooms* and methamphetamine. By 20, she had become a homeless heroin addict who lived out of a car with her boyfriend.

However, middle-aged women—white women, in particular—are the group of people with the highest risk of death from opioid addiction. From 1999 to 2014 the death rate due to drug use jumped 400 percent for this subgroup. Middle-aged women are being prescribed opioids for a variety of reasons, including chronic pain due to injuries, menopause, fibromyalgia, lupus, and depression and anxiety.

Karen Franklin of Bakersfield, California is one of those women. At age 43 she received a prescription for Vicodin to deal with the pain of an injury. Soon, she was taking the medication regularly and found herself dealing with the drug's side effects. These included anxiety, sleeplessness, and depression. Her job at a grocery store involved heavy lifting and that caused her injury to get worse. She asked her doctor for stronger medicine. Prescriptions for codeine, oxycodone, and

OxyContin followed. Now 60 years old, she smokes cigarettes and chases down a dozen different medications with vodka. No longer able to work, she began to suffer from new health problems like pancreatitis and irritable bowel syndrome. Her friend Ellen Eggert describes her condition as "a slow suicide." Franklin agrees that her habits are not healthy, but she refuses treatment for addiction. Soon, she may become another lethal statistic due to opioid addiction.

Drug Use and Others

When one person in a family is a drug addict, everyone suffers. This includes parents, brothers, sisters, grandparents, and anyone else in the home. Addicts may lie or steal to get money for drugs. They may lose their jobs, disappear for days at a time, and neglect their responsibilities to family members.

Drug addicts often resist the idea that they have a disease that needs treatment. Fights may become frequent, and law enforcement might enter the picture. In 2013, the Partnership for Drug-Free Kids reported that drug use is involved in 80 percent of child abuse cases, 50 percent of violent crimes, and 50 percent of *domestic violence* incidents.

Families and friends of addicts are not the only ones affected. The National Institute on Drug Abuse estimates that abuse of illicit drugs costs the US almost $200 billion per year due to crime, loss of work productivity, and medical care.

Criminal Justice and Opioid Addiction

The FBI reports approximately 1.6 million drug-related arrests each year. This is a larger number than arrests for theft, assault, driving under the influence (DUI), and every other category except property crimes. Punishment of drug addicts often veers between *incarceration* and treatment. The establishment of drug courts is an attempt by the criminal justice system to offer people convicted of drug offenses to obtain community-based treatment. Such treatment is supervised closely by the courts and offers participants a means of avoid-

Sex, Drugs, and Opioids

A study published in the *Journal of Interpersonal Violence* found that opioid users often encounter a "quid pro quo" (this for that) expectation regarding sex. Seventy-three percent of women and 49 percent of men reported that they had been in situations where someone expected them to have sex because of the drug use they were engaging in together. The study's lead author, Lauren Jessell, reported, "When drugs were provided free of cost to potential partners, there was an expectation that those receiving the drugs would provide sexual favors in return."

In most cases, the study found that men were expected to have sex with other men while women were expected to have sex with men as well. Opioid users who refused sex for drugs were at risk for harassment and assault. While conducting interviews with the research participants, Jessell notes that the study personnel "were taken aback by how often we discovered they were involved in sexual violence."

A separate study of young adults, conducted by New York University's College of Nursing, found that 41 percent of young adult females and 11 percent of young adult males reported that they were forced into sex while using opioids.

US Drug Schedules

In the United States, drugs are placed into five categories, known as schedules, to help identify risk of abuse and dependency as well as suggested medical use, if any, for the drug. Schedule 1 drugs, such as ecstasy, heroin and LSD, are considered the most dangerous drugs of all. These drugs have a high potential for abuse and are not accepted for medical use. Schedule II drugs include cocaine, oxycodone, fentanyl, methadone and Adderall, which all carry a high potential for abuse and can cause serious physical or psychological dependence.

Schedule III drugs include ketamine and Tylenol with codeine, which have a moderate to low potential for physical and psychological dependence. Schedule IV drugs, such as Tramadol, Xanax, Valium and Ambien, have a low potential for abuse and dependency. Schedule V drugs, such as cough syrups with under 200 milligrams of codeine, contain limited amounts of specific narcotics and have the lowest potential for abuse.

ing prison time for their offenses. The courts represent a joint effort by the judicial system, drug treatment providers, and other community groups to improve both public health and public safety. They have been operating for more than 20 years in the US.

The government estimates that for every $1 spent on drug courts, there are more than $2 in savings to the criminal justice system by itself. Today there are more than 2,500 drug courts, serving about 120,000 cases each year. A Department of Justice study found that 84 percent of individuals who had graduated from drug courts had not been arrested for serious crimes in the following year. Follow-up at the two-year mark showed 72.5 percent had no further arrests.

Not all places have drug-court programs, however. The most recent figures indicate that about 47 percent of counties in the US offer government drug courts.

Text-Dependent Questions

1. What has been the stereotype of heroin addicts in the past? How is it different today?
2. List some of the differences between men and women when it comes to the effects opioids have on their bodies.
3. What is the purpose of drug courts and how effective are they?

Research Project

By contacting local law enforcement and criminal justice agencies, or by accessing information available on websites and in official publications, ask about the use of drug courts in your state or province. If they are not available in your area, ask about programs designed to keep offenders off drugs and out of prisons. Write several paragraphs about your findings.

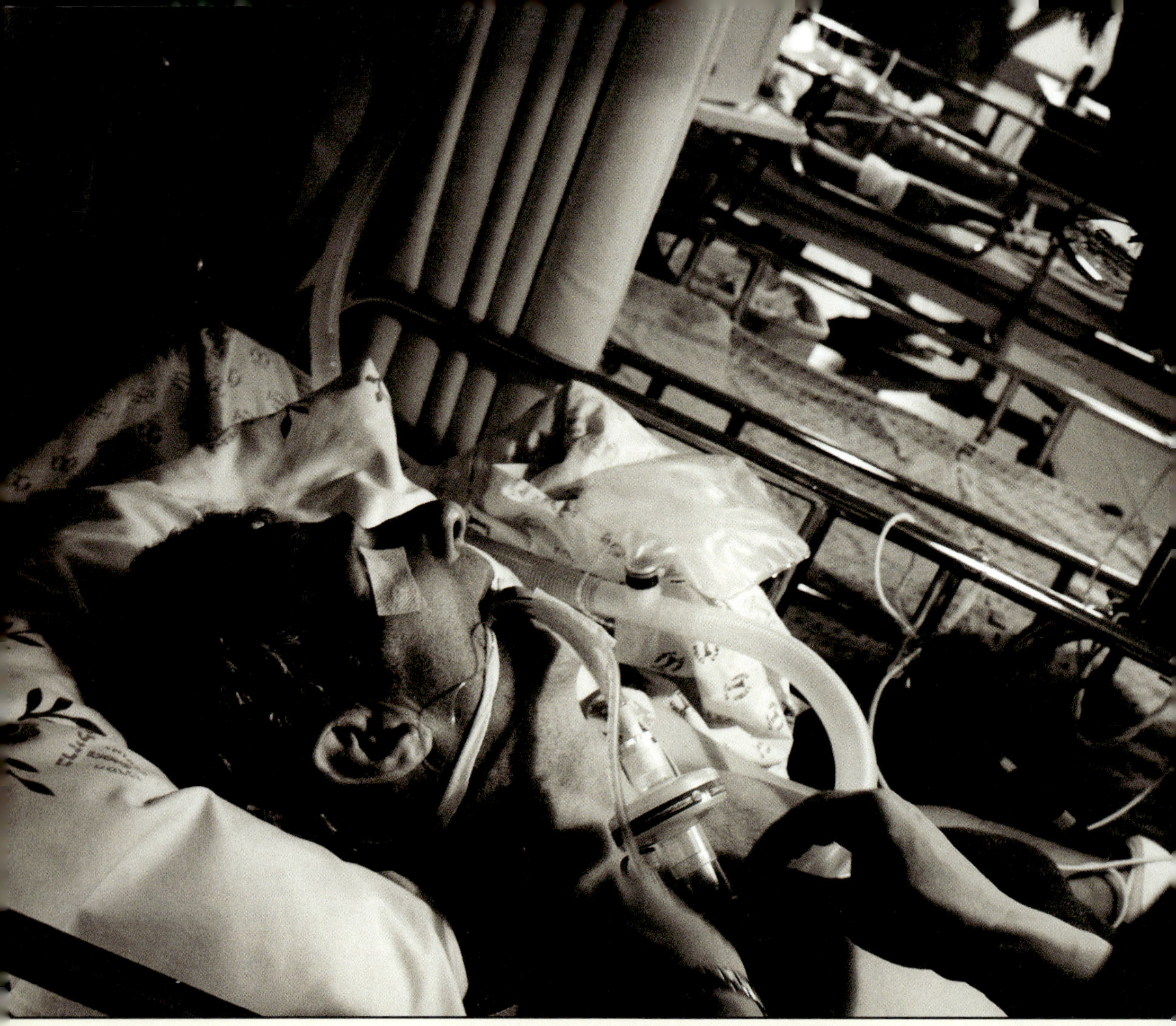

 **Words to Understand in This Chapter**

detoxification—a program that specializes in treating the medical needs of persons in withdrawal. Also known as detox.

outpatient—medical or emotional treatment outside of a medical facility.

stigma—negative beliefs a society has about something.

A drug addict undergoes a rapid opioid detoxification treatment in a clinic. Such a treatment is an effective method of getting people off drugs in the short term, but other programs are required to make sure that they do not relapse into addiction.

Over and Through Addiction

It's true. The facts about opioid use and abuse are grim. The health consequences are serious, just like those to immediate friends and family and society at large. But there is a way out. Treatment is complex, though. No single treatment will work for all affected individuals. It must address all of the person's needs, not just their drug use.

Initially, the addict does not even need to enter a treatment program voluntarily for eventual success. The most important aspect is long-term commitment to work on the physical, mental, emotional, and spiritual dimensions of addiction. Treatment must help the person stop using drugs, stay off them in the future, and become a productive member of a family, the job market, and society at large.

Successful Treatment

The first step in dealing with addiction is *detoxification*, also known as detox. Detox is the process of removing the drug from the body. When the addict ceases drug use, symptoms of withdrawal occur. Medications can help with these symptoms. A 2014 study by SAMHSA reveals that medications were used in 80 percent of drug detoxes. It's not hard to see why. During withdrawal, people experience body aches, pain in the abdomen, diarrhea, nausea, vomiting, chills and goose bumps, large pupils, anxiety, mood swings, and an intense craving for drugs. Most people will do anything to avoid these symptoms, which last from hours to several days, and even weeks.

Methadone is the most effective treatment for narcotic addiction because it is a long-acting opioid itself. It eases symptoms and cravings but its use does not provide the opioid rush. Over time the dosage can be tapered off, though some people elect to remain on a maintenance dosage. While remaining on such a dosage is not ridding users of opioids, it does have certain advantages. Methadone is distributed in a medical clinic, allowing the user to hold down a job and achieve some stability in life, a condition that is difficult, if not downright impossible, for active opioid addicts.

Buprenorphine can be used alone, like brand name Subutex, or with the addition of naloxone, with brand name drug Suboxone. Both drugs reduce cravings and withdrawal symptoms. Usually, Subutex is used for detox. Suboxone is used either for detox or maintenance as prevention for a relapse into addiction again.

Clonidine is a blood pressure medication. It acts on the

From Down and Out to Clean and Sober

Lisa Guerrieri seemed like a normal Levittown, Pennsylvania high school student. She liked to smoke pot sometimes, and take pills other times. She never counted on becoming a heroin addict. In fact, she couldn't believe she was herself the first time she injected it. But it became all too real when she quickly became addicted. Her family—a loving mother, stepfather, and older sister—had no idea that she had a problem. At first, that was. It wasn't long before her problem escalated.

Her family sent her to rehab clinics nine times. Each time she left rehab she stayed clean for a little while, but inevitably relapsed. Lisa said, "I used in my room. I used in my car. I used in every room in this house. I would go into rehab, and my mom and stepdad would take me back."

While she was using drugs, Lisa met a pimp. He offered her free heroin if she would post her picture on the internet. It wasn't long before she and other high school girls from the suburbs were arrested for prostitution. The pimp would keep the cash the girls' earned and provide them with enough heroin to keep them highly addicted. She spent nine days in jail where she withdrew from heroin cold turkey. When she got out she entered rehab again. This time she graduated from a program.

"Now I have a really good life," she reported. "I wake up and I feel like a human. I have a job, I pay my bills. I have things in my apartment that I'm not going to pawn."

brain to reduce the "fight or flight" response, which withdrawal magnifies. It does not reduce cravings, however.

Some private programs referred to as rapid detox give patients large doses of these drugs. Others place the patient under general anesthesia. Such programs are not any more effective than traditional detox methods. They may be more dangerous, in fact.

Behavioral Therapies

Initial detox from opioids is not enough for most people to remain free from addiction. Relapse, or returning to a state of active drug addiction, is common. In addition to the medicines already mentioned, naltrexone, or brand name Vivitrol, is also used to prevent relapse. It blocks the effects of opioids at the receptor level. Naltrexone should only be used on detoxified individuals.

Because the risk of relapse is so high after initial detox, counseling and other behavioral therapies are strongly recommended as well. These therapies are designed to help patients to change behaviors and attitudes that relate to drug use, to

 **Did You Know?**

Narcotics Anonymous, or NA, was formed in 1947. It followed the the model of the highly effective twelve-step program Alcoholics Anonymous. Today there are about 20,000 weekly NA meetings in 70 countries.

Over and Through Addiction 53

Twelve-step programs like Narcotics Anonymous often include a group therapy component, in which recovering addicts can share their stories and experiences with others and receive support and encouragement.

establish healthy skills for coping with life. They are designed to work with other kinds of treatment such as medication. Participants can use them while in a rehab facility, also called residential treatment (inpatient) or on an outpatient basis.

Inpatient treatment can be highly effective. It can also be expensive. There are several kinds of types, from 24-hour a day medical facilities which keep patients for 6-12 months to shorter term program and recovery houses that provides short-term, supervised places for patients to live in while they transition into a drug-free life.

Outpatient treatment involves different types of counseling and therapy. One kind is cognitive-based therapy. It helps patients recognize situations that might lead to them using drugs, and work to avoid them or cope with them. Family therapy is often used for young people still living at home. It helps to improve family life on multiple levels.

One of the most popular self-help programs is Narcotics Anonymous, or NA, used in almost three-fourths of treatment centers. This program involves outpatient meetings in local areas, inpatient meetings in rehabs, and even gatherings in prisons and hospitals. Often intensive participation is recommended, even up to attending one or more meetings per day. NA is called a twelve-step program. The twelve steps are a series of principles that members adhere to in order to achieve a drug-free lifestyle. The program is not religious, but rather spiritual in nature. A person's specific religion or lack of religion is not important in the program. Instead, it promotes a method of healing that involves surrender to a higher power than the person themselves. Personal stories and support from other recovering addicts are key to the program, which provides a set of tools to help individuals live drug-free.

 **Educational Video**

To learn some facts about addiction that may surprise you, scan here:

Mental Illness

A history of mental illness, many times undiagnosed, leads many people into a life of opioid addiction. NAMI, the National Alliance on Mental Illness, reports that more than half of all drug addicts also experience some form of mental illness. A person with both mental illness and drug addiction is said to have a dual diagnosis. Treatment for mental illness is necessary in addition to other forms of addiction-related activities. Examples of mental illnesses include depression, bipolar disorder, anxiety disorders, schizophrenia, and others. While sufferers of mental illnesses often find themselves to be victims of a stigma against diseases of the mind, attitudes are improving as education about these disorders becomes more widespread.

Symptoms of mental illness may vary greatly. Often they include the person isolating themselves from others, experiencing a persistent low mood, showing significant changes in energy levels, and/or believing untrue things, known as delusions, or seeing or hearing things that others don't, known as hallucinations.

How to Help an Addict

By reading this book, you now know the signs, symptoms, and dangers of opioid and opiate use and abuse. But what if you know a friend or family member that has a problem? Often friends and loved ones of addicts try to help them with problems created by the addiction. They hand over money, provide a place to stay, look for a job for them, watch their children, and so on. While on the surface this is a loving act, underneath

You can support a friend or family member who is dealing with a drug problem by encouraging them to receive treatment, but you cannot force an addict to change. The drug-addicted person must accept responsibility for his or her actions in order to truly recover.

it is something else: enabling. To enable an addict is to keep them from the consequences of their actions. Stopping to enable an addict is a form of tough love, one that is extremely difficult for most people. It is also necessary for your own well-being and in order to keep you from feeding into another's addictive behaviors.

The unexpected answer to the question of how to help an addict is to care for yourself. By caring for yourself you are able to offer proper support to your loved one in a way that keeps from enabling their behavior and that keeps you from being dragged down into the chaos of an addict's existence. This does not mean to separate yourself from the person, but instead to find support for yourself. One way to do this is to visit Nar-Anon, a twelve-step program for friends and family members of a narcotics addicts. It is similar to Narcotics Anonymous except that it is specifically geared toward the challenges, difficulties, and experiences that only other loved ones of addicts can understand. At Nar-Anon meetings you will find a community of others who have experienced many of the same things that you have, and provide vital support to you.

Text-Dependent Questions

1. Why is detox a necessary step in addiction treatment?
2. What are some reasons why behavioral therapies are necessary for most addicts?
3. How do you think that having a mental illness affects the chances that someone will become an addict?

Research Project

Using the internet, look for resources in your area for supporting and helping friends and family members of addicts. Compile a list of five activities. Think outside the box as you do so. This may mean including organizations like volunteer groups, charities, or faith communities on your list.

# Series Glossary

analgesic—any member of a class of drugs used to achieve analgesia, or relief from pain.

central nervous system—the part of the human nervous system that consists of the brain and spinal cord. These are greatly affected by opiates and opioids.

dependence—a situation that occurs when opiates or opioids are used so much that the user's body adapts to the drug and only functions normally when the drug is present. When the user attempts to stop using the drug, a physiologic reaction known as withdrawal syndrome occurs.

epidemic—a widespread occurrence of a disease or illness in a community at a particular time.

opiates—a drug that is derived directly from the poppy plant, such as opium, heroin, morphine, and codeine.

opioids—synthetic drugs that affect the body in a similar way as opiate drugs. The opioids include Oxycotin, hydrocodone, fentanyl, and methadone.

withdrawal—a syndrome of often painful physical and psychological symptoms that occurs when someone stops using an addictive drug, such as an opiate or opioid. Often, the drug user will begin taking the drug again to avoid withdrawal.

Further Reading

Gammill, Joani. *Painkillers, Heroin, and the Road to Sanity*. Center City, MN: Hazelden, 2014.

Knight, A.J. *Opiate Withdrawal: How to Kick Opiates, Cure Your Addiction And Make it Through the Detox Withdrawals*. CreateSpace, 2015.

Sheff, David. *Clean: Overcoming Addiction and Ending America's Greatest Tragedy*. New York: Houghton Mifflin Harcourt, 2013.

Vest, David. *Making Millions, Making Monsters: My Experience Working in the Field of Opiate Replacement Therapy*. Amazon, 2014.

Wiles, Justin. *Through an Addict's Eyes: Day in the Life of an Addict*. Amazon, 2017.

Internet Resources

www.cdc.gov/drugoverdose/prescribing/patients.html

The CDC maintains a webpage with helpful information for patients who are prescribed opioids to learn about the drugs and dangers associated with them.

www.ccsa.ca

This website delivers a wide range of publications on substance abuse in Canada. Subjects relate to prescription drugs, alcohol, youths, treatment, impaired driving, prevention, and standards—among others.

www.samhsa.gov

A vast amount of research related to opioids and other substances can be performed on the Substance Abuse and Mental Health Services Administration website. The website also provides resources on national strategies and initiatives, state and local initiatives, and training and education.

Publisher's Note: The websites listed on these pages were active at the time of publication. The publisher is not responsible for websites that have changed their address or discontinued operation since the date of publication. The publisher reviews and updates the websites each time the book is reprinted.

www.dea.gov/druginfo/factsheets.shtml

>The Drug Enforcement Administration (DEA) maintains fact sheets on numerous narcotics, hallucinogens, stimulants, depressants, and other drugs of concern.

www.drugfreeworld.org/real-life-stories/heroin.html

>The Foundation for a Drug-Free World provides a video and real life quotes from heroin addicts.

https://easyread.drugabuse.gov/

>The National Institute on Drug Abuse maintains a webpage called Easy-to-Read Drug Facts that contains short videos, drug profiles, and personal stories of teens in recovery.

www.nar-anon.org/

>Nar-Anon is a 12-step program for the families and friends of addicts with meetings all over the world.

www.painmed.org/

>The American Academy of Pain Medicine's website provides current and relevant information on pain medicine, including clinical reference resources and the latest news on pain research.

www.cihi.ca/en

>The Canadian Institute for Health Information website offers a National Prescription Drug Utilization Information System (NPDUIS) Database that stores pan-Canadian information on public drug programs.

Index

Actiq lollipop, 26
addiction, 7–11, 15, 23, 24, **39**, 40–43
    and arrests, 44–46, 47
    costs of, 8, 44
    and enabling behaviors, 55–57
    and family life, 39–40, 44
    and helping addicts, 55–57
    and mental illness, 55
    and overdose deaths, 8–10, 43
    and prescription drugs, 33–34, 36–37, **39**, 43–44
    and sexual favors, 45
    and women, 41–44
    See also opioids; treatment, addiction
American Academy of Pain Management, **32**
American Pain Society, **32**
animal cruelty, 30
arrests, drug, 44–46, 47
atarax, 19

Bailey, Chad, 30
behavioral therapies, 52–53
black tar heroin, 7, 21–22
    See also heroin
Brennan, Connor, 34–36
buprenorphine, 19, 50

China, 14, 37
clonidine, 50, 52
codeine, 16, 19, 20, **21**, 43, 46
Columbus, Christopher, 14
Comey, James B., 40–41
Controlled Substances Act, 32

DeGroote, Jacob, 7–8
DeGroote, Mari, 8
demerol, 19
dentists, 33, 34
    See also physicians
"Deon," 39–40
detoxification (detox), 48, **49**, 50, 52
    See also treatment, addiction
dilaudid, 19
"doctor shopping," 23
    See also physicians
domestic violence, 38, 44
Dreamland: The Story of America's New Opiate Epidemic (Quinones), 37
drug courts, 45–47
drug-seeking, 30

Eggert, Ellen, 44
endogenous opioids, 17
endorphins, 17

fentanyl, 9, 19, 25–27, 37, 46
Franklin, Karen, 43–44

generic drugs, 18, 19–20
    See also prescriptions
Guerrieri, Lisa, 51

Hatzell, James, 33
heroin, 14, 15, 19, 21–23, **26**, 27, 37,

Numbers in ***bold italic*** refer to captions.

40, 46, 51
  black tar, 7, 21–22
  and overdose deaths, 8
  street names for, 35
  and women, 41
Hibpshman, Micah, 30
hydrocodine, 19
hydrocodone (Vicodin), **19**, 20, 32, 33, 43
hydromorphone, 19, 23–24, 35

Janssen, Paul, 25
Jessell, Lauren, 45

Landry, Blake, 43
laudanum, 14
  See also opium
lortab, 19

marijuana, 20, 34, 37, 43
McKesson, 31–32
mental illness, 55
methadone, 19, 24, 35, 46, 50
methamphetamine, 18, 20, 43
Mexico, **31**, 37
morphine, 14, 16, 19, 20–21, 23, 27, 35
mushrooms (shrooms), 38, 43

naloxone, 19, 50
naltrexone, 19, 52
Nar Anon, 57
narcotics, 12, 13–14, 16, 19–20
  marketing of, **32**, 33
  See also opioids
Narcotics Anonymous (NA), 40, 52, **53**, 54, 57
norco, 10
noscapine (narcotine), 16

Obama, Barack, 10
opiates, 43
  definition of, 16
opioids
  and animal prescriptions, 30
  and the brain, 16–17

definition of, 15–16
and drug schedules, 46
and overdose deaths, 6, **7**, 8–10, 20, 21, 23, 24, 25, 27, **29**, 35–36, 43
and prescription guidelines, 34
synthetic, 16, 19, 24–25
types of, 19–27, 35
withdrawal symptoms from, 15, 16, 24, 50
and women, 41–44
See also addiction; prescriptions; individual opioid names
opium, 13–14, 20, 35
opium alkaloids, 16
opium poppies, 13–16, 19, 21, 37
Opium Wars, 14
orpivaine, 19
overdoses, drug, 6, 9, 20, 21, 24, 25, 27
  heroin, 23, 35–36
  number of, **7**, 8–10, **29**, 43
oxycodone, 24–25, 29–30, 32, 35, 43, 46
OxyContin, 19, 20, 24, **25**, 34, 44
oxymorphone, 19

papaverine, 16
Percocet, 33
Pereira, Heather D., 30
pharmaceutical industry, 28
  and illegal drug sales, 31–32
  and marketing, **32**, 33
  See also prescriptions
physicians
  and opioid prescriptions, 23, 33–34
poppies (opium), 13–16, 19, 21, 37
Prescription Opioid and Heroin Epidemic Awareness Week, 10
prescriptions, 8
  and addiction, 33–34, 36–37, **39**, 43–44
  and fraud, 23, 26–27, 29–30, 32–33
  number of, 26, 33–34
  and women, **42**, 43–44

Prince, 9
Prosper, Alejandro, 29–30, 31

Quinones, Sam, 37

receptors, opioid, 16, 17
rehab, 6, 8, 51, 53
    See also treatment, addiction
relapse, 28, 36, 52
    See also treatment, addiction
research projects, 11, 17, 27, 37, 47, 57

schedules, drug, 46
semisynthetic drugs, 18, 19
sexual favors, 45
shrooms (mushrooms), 38, 43
street names, drug, 35
Suboxone, 50
Subutex, 50
Sydenham, Thomas, 14

thebaine, 16, 19

Tramadol, 30, 46
treatment, addiction, 35, 40, 49–52, 55–57
    and behavioral therapies, 52–53
    and cognitive-based therapy, 54
    and detoxification, 48, **49**, 50, 52
    and drug courts, 45–46
    and mental illness, 55
    and Narcotics Anonymous (NA), 40, 52, **53**, 54, 57
    and rehab, 6, 8, 51, 53
    and relapse, 28, 36, 52
    with synthetic opioids, 19, 24, 50
    See also addiction

Vicodin (hydrocodone), **19**, 20, 32, 33, 43
Vivitrol (naltrexone), 19, 52

Walker, Madison, 35–36
withdrawal symptoms, 15, 16, 24, 50

About the Author

Xina M. Uhl is an educational writer and the author of more than twenty nonfiction books. Before becoming a full-time writer, she worked in substance abuse recovery treatment programs for Maricopa County Government in Phoenix, Arizona. She makes her home in southern California where she enjoys hiking with her three dogs.

Picture Credits: DEA photo: 19, 22, 25, 26; courtesy Ebby Lowry Photography, http://ebbylphotographyblog.com: 6; © OTTN Publishing: 10; used under license from Shutterstock, Inc.: 1, 12, 28, 32, 36, 38, 41, 42, 53, 56; ChameleonsEye / Shutterstock.com: 48; Jack Dagley Photography / Shutterstock.com: 31; United Nations photo: 21.